Scared Gods

Joseph M. Lopez

All rights reserved. No part of this book may be reproduced or transmitted in any form or by any means, electronic or mechanical, including photocopying, recording, or by an information storage and retrieval system - except by a reviewer who may quote brief passages in a review to be printed in a magazine or newspaper – without permission in writing from the publisher.

-Writer Heights Publishing

-This Book is Dedicated to my big little city

(Sturgeon Bay)

and

the people who make it sound.

Intro

There are

moments we live-

and moments

we cause.

TABLE OF CONTENTS

11	Three Hundred and Ninety-Five
12	The Meat and Potatoes of It
13	Milkshake
14 -15	Zero Minus Zero
16	Moxie and Truth
17	An Awkward Walk
18	Merely Beautiful
19	Someone Similar
20	The Path of Least Resistance
21	Occupied
22	Where the World Met
23	A Gray Undertaking
24	Chance and Luck
25	I Concede
26	Equally Unsure
27	Scissors, Children, and Wind Chimes
28	Voice Message From Greg
29	It Is Blue
30	Like and Love
31	Prayers Pinned
32	Captive and Aware
33	A Most Exquisite Dance
34	And So It Goes
35	Encanto

36	The Color of Proof
37	Alfred Hitchcock Got It Wrong
38	More Than That
39	Italian Ice
40	Frayed
41	Nothing
42	Anchoring
43	Feed the Lake
44	Lost to You
45	Lilacs and Bees
46	Bark of the Black Dog
47	Breath of the Dead
48	You and the Moon
49	Soon
50	Queer and Brown
51	A Quiet Place
52	Aching to Bloom
53	Until You Tell Me
54	This Burn
55	I'll Find Another
56	Kryptonite
57	It Is Raining Strawberries
58	Linda
59	Life
60	Deliverance
61	Lost to Her

62	Familia
63	No More Magic
64	Going Back
65	Fishing
66	Canadian Serenade (In Blue)
67	Sturgeon Bay
68	A Hearse of my Own
69	Songs I Don't Yet Know
70	And I Love
71	Poetic Neglect
72	I Hope You Don't Mind
73	People Like Us
74	Never Beige
75	Prone
76	4:07 PM
77	Familiar Friend
78	Bigger Than
79	A Curious Shade
80	Bare
81	Planets In Conjunction
82	We Are
83	This Dance Between Friends
84	Oil and Rain and Rain
85	Willingly
86	The Length of Youth
87	The Aries

88	Beautiful and Smart
89	To Measure You By
90	A Name Returned
91	This Thing We Carry
92	No Because Yes
93	Scared Gods
94	The Alphabet Game
95	Intrigued
96	Walked Intentions
97	Firmer Than Water
98-99	Not Just Yet
100	Even Dogs Know
101	The Dare
102	Sleeping Under Water
103	All I Know
104-106	Learning You
107	Seventeen Miles
108	Marked In Proper
109	The Weight of My Worth

Commence...

I will only ask

three hundred

and ninety-five

more times

who you are.

You can't right now.

I can.

I'd like to.

I'd like to discuss

the meat and potatoes of it

over a dinner of pasta and shrimp.

I'll tell what this feeling is.

The why.

You do the same.

You say it exists.

So do I.

You want to run.

And I want to at least say goodbye.

And none of this-

before I knew you existed.

We could.

You are a few miles away.

My feet

face west on my bed.

I follow the sun with them.

I follow the day.

I've already walked past morning-

and it is snowing again.

One of the last this spring.

The bare maple

is traced against the gray

of this Monday sky.

And I trace with my eyes

the still bare maple.

I cannot see the sun

behind the afternoon.

And all I want right now-

is to drink a milkshake alone.

You asked if I'd been to the woods of Canada-

or Alaska.

I hadn't.

You imagined them as unfiltered Wisconsin.

I tend to agree.

But I don't know this any more than you.

Than the illusion and perception we build of these-

and us.

So we begin, discussing the things we know.

And this scares us.

A conversation about the equation of nothing.

We philosophize.

Trees and god.

You, and me.

The readiness of anyone to move into the space of another.

That we are one.

The stars, the sky, the things we breathe.

The streets we walk.

That maybe the punishment of humans, is the awareness of this.

Que the panic.

That we are no greater or less than.

And if that should bring us comfort.

That no matter what-

zero plus zero-

or zero minus zero-

is always zero.

It is always the number we agree on.

Even if birth and death are nothing.

And the middle is nothing.

That's an extra zero.

But I argue that we should find pleasure in the middle.

Something small-

something ordinary.

I tell you to say the word-

and I will get you.

You say you will reach out for me soon.

I say goodnight-

sleep well.

And I say let's call this space beautiful.

I liked the way you looked at the night sky.

in its clearness, its darkness-

declaring it beautiful.

My eyes agreed.

And my eyes fell from the sky-

down to the place we stood.

Back to your skin, to the tangible-

the possible.

We wore the same shade of brown-

a label of our birth.

You brought yourself daringly.

You questioned my eyes, and the dark.

We understood its starkness.

Hungry eyes, and starved lips.

We feasted.

We fed the night, and each other.

My lips on your lips, your fingers in my mouth.

And we were the definition of moxie and truth in a moment.

It's raining today.

I think each sky drop speaks your name.

My thoughts fall and pool

with the afternoon.

They are of you.

We are

an awkward walk-

fumbling over words.

One, assembling the next.

Keeping pace

with a night that chose us.

When I tell you

it is beautiful here-

I mean to say-

is this heart-

occupied by your feet.

Without you-

yes-

without you-

life

is merely beautiful.

Say the word.

I'll come for you

on Sunday.

You can be god-

or someone similar.

Who lived in Apartment N.

I tore apart

the English language-

chasing rain.

To find-

that in November and March

the rain speaks the same.

That emptied fields

understand fog in winter.

They know the path

of least resistance-

the one of coyote and deer.

Not the hearts of men.

And that I understand the thoughts of a small town-

stapled with cars.

The sounds of Third Avenue after 9 pm.

And Fourth.

And a sky that weeps people at night.

And I found-

that the lake and I

are hungry-

that we can only sleep

when fed.

There are things in life

that stick.

I mean to say

that this heart of mine-

is somehow occupied

by the face

and feet

of you.

The world met

in those yellow walls

and fat checkered floors-

in black and white.

Under that red tin roof-

and red doors.

Shaded in the afternoon-

guarded in heart by me.

Olga and Misha-

Nicole and Petr.

The world posed-

wearing warm regard.

Faces and friendship-

philosophies and love.

Hearts meeting hearts.

Acquired

and arranged in oils.

It began in the rain.

This   walk.

Saturday felt our feet.

Her sidewalks rubbed-

on a very

downtown afternoon.

Third Avenue-

and Fourth.

A gray undertaking.

A decided walk.

One to decide

what we felt like

under these skies.

I smell like you-

and Saturdays rain.

Still.

The lingering of a game

of chance and luck-

and conversation

that crawled the brick walls

of downtown buildings.

And the streets

that learned how we sound

walking together.

Our names.

The thoughts we offered-

And a close and crooked smile.

One of unexpected ease.

For root beer-

and company.

And Sunday strung

on a breath of April.

For gentle curiosity

in understanding

what I meant.

And for lips-

and for hands-

that agree with mine.

For days and hours

lost to ease.

I concede.

Set me out

at the start of April-

where light and I

are equally unsure.

Where we are softly-

and equally unsteady.

Where we search for balance-

to begin the walk

using the sound

of our forgotten

wintered feet.

A week later

and my hands fit better in yours.

I tested this theory.

After you showed me

the Fresnel lens

overlooking the Strawberry Islands-

and laughing at a few early tourists

walking suspiciously close

to hungry waters.

I tested this theory

after we talked to Angela-

about scissors, children, and wind chimes.

After I insisted

a yellow square candle

became yours.

A week later-

and my hands know yours better.

I tested this theory.

I pace the deck-

coffee in hand-

watching Wednesday.

Unmovable morning fog.

Your voice lends itself to me-

through the poem you left

as a voice message

as I slept.

I pace the peeling deck-

leaning into the brilliance

of your words.

And I hold my phone

close to my ear-

not wanting to share your words

with anyone.

Not with the birds.

Not with the ridge.

Not with April.

And certainly not the fog.

My favorite color

is blue.

I answered a Saturday question

on Sunday.

Not as dark as the Jeep

parked in the driveway.

And not the blue

of the metal snow shovel

I meant to put away.

It is April.

It is the blue

of the sweater I wore

with the brown corduroys

on our first date.

It is that very blue.

I'm lost-

somewhere between

the shore

and the horizon.

Between like

and love.

And I only speak that way

about you-

and the lake.

Prayers are being hung on me.

And I feel their weight.

More so as I age.

Heavier-

because I look like my father.

I am aware.

I am the hope

of my cousins and aunties.

I am their name.

I am the name of my father.

I am aware.

It is also mine.

And that I am the entirety

of my ancestors

and their dreams.

I do read the prayers

pinned to me.

I feel the love.

I pray I am enough.

I find myself grinning

like a fool

when the thought of you

insists itself on my brain.

It happens more now.

A month ago, you didn't exist.

A month ago

I didn't know

you do that thing with your eyes

when you pretend

someone doesn't annoy you.

I smile-

because I know this now.

And to the fact

that I'm captive.

And aware.

I smile-

and I don't care

That the people I pass downtown

see.

I do that in front of you.

A spider

in the mouth-

requires

a most

exquisite

dance of the

tongue.

You.

And me.

We move differently.

Not bound by convention.

We walk easy

in the company

of the other.

In the knowledge

that we are falling.

And so it goes.

We never wrote that poem-

the one about the moon.

Not yet.

And we argue

whether she is one

who will listen-

or simply stare cold.

But we had the lake today-

and a smile on a woman's face

when she saw us

walking out of the woods

holding hands.

And you. And I. Smiled.

But you have Encanto-

and three kinds of peanut butter.

One for each mood.

I wear blues

and greens-

and speak of May-

as though she should be Queen.

I dream of her

in colors

she has yet to prove.

It happened today.

The unintended.

There was so much joy in the day.

We laughed fully at Kewaunee Custard and Grill.

And again when you picked out that blue pig for my dog-

you squeaked it the whole time we shopped.

And we smiled on our way home-

watching the woman make the face she did

while riding her bicycle uphill on Mathey Road.

The miles between the counties south-

and the County of Door, were filled with joy.

That space was sacred.

We measured the distance in smiles, laughing in lumens.

Saying that Alfred Hitchcock may have gotten it wrong.

It shouldn't have been The Birds-

but pillars of bugs by the lake.

And when we got to my house I cried.

The years and thoughts-

And the weight of the things I carry, I gave you.

You took them with grace-

the things I never speak.

You held me and I sighed-

letting me know it is ok to breathe.

That it is time to breathe.

It as though I cannot breathe

when you are not in sight.

That the ground

is asking for my knees.

Like when you had to go tonight.

I

I could simply say

I miss you.

It's more than that.

It's that I know now

how much

our noses and foreheads

pressed together-

say everything we need.

To be aware

of where we are.

After finishing

our Italian ice.

Standing-

in your kitchen.

Standing in awe.

I stared.

But so did you.

I suddenly said

I had to go.

And forced myself

to act on those words.

I drove

the   lengthy mile   home.

Then texted-

that I missed you already.

You texted the same.

Of cherry blossoms

and dandelions-

and bees that learn

the sound of May.

Of daffodils

and tulips

in soil that breaths

the length of day.

Of the fall

of the kingdom of winter-

and how we walk in.

Frayed

from the weight of a season

stayed

in patience-

waiting for word

from the sun.

I told you-

I'm falling for you.

You said

you didn't do anything.

And that's just it.

Nothing is required.

It is for you being you

in this space we share.

And for allowing me

to do the same.

I set down

my oars.

I chose

to anchor

to the shores

you walk.

Feed the rain

to this lake.

Feed her the sky.

Feed her my boat

and thoughts-

and oars

and hands.

Give her these.

Let her hunger

know my name.

Feed her my eyes.

Sink my feet

to these shores.

She is my life

and grave.

Tonight-

I sit with what I told you.

With the fact

that you followed me

out of the shower

and into my bedroom-

and simply held me.

And I was lost to you

Then to the kitchen-

after watching me dress-

where we prepared potatoes and steaks for the grill.

Where-

in this kitchen

you pulled me close.

And again, I was lost to you.

I said as much.

These eyes meeting yours-

can no longer hide this.

Today

I smelled summer.

She walked in

unexpected-

wearing lilacs and bees.

And I welcomed her-

as I always have.

I'm screaming at you

from the deck.

And in the front yard

the purple iris

stands tall.

You are yelling back at me-

and the birds sing

to the sun

that finally showed itself.

The black dog

barks

at the very same rabbit

He sees each evening.

I understand his bark.

We are

all of us-

looking at the same big sky.

From our awkward birth

until the day we die.

Building our fragile lives-

telling ourselves

we can measure eternity

under the Milky Way.

Keeping ourselves-

and each other company.

Watching fat moons rise-

and stars stumbling.

Breathing the breath

of the dead-

in exchange

for a determinate future.

And here we all are.

I feel them.

These nuanced pulls.

Only something

you

and the moon

can do.

I am dreaming-

under this sky-

of the places

I am soon to wander.

I am queer-

and brown.

And the lake doesn't mind.

Neither do the trees.

I don't need much-

not-

in the way of things.

Give me

                              the corner of a

                sofa

                        and a mug of

            Chai Tea.

                        I'll write us the

              world.

Give me a quiet place

to lay my thoughts-

d i l u t e d-

by afternoon sun.

Grant me

the sound of your smile

and the grasp of your hand.

With

your nose to mine.

Simply said-

it is enough-

the skin of you-

on the skin of me.

Walk with me.

Our bare feet in June-

naked-

to June.

Susceptible to her ways.

Past the lilacs

held with purpose

and a wink.

To the pregnant Strawberry moon-

regarded as Queen.

On this we agree.

And the pink peonies lining the drive-

aching to bloom.

To the birds at bath-

and the dogs that call them

each by name.

Through fields the fireflies claim

solely as their own.

Walk with me through June.

Slow-

through a season we press to.

Occupied

in heart and ease.

I'm here

to write you

poems of

                                        love-

until you tell me

otherwise.

It is late June-

and I watch

as fireflies ignite

an expectant field.

One that has waited

for this solstice-

this burn.

I look at the lilac that I will never view

in the same way again.

And my favorite apple tree.

Perhaps I'll find another.

And the nest, and the scream of the killdeer,

that I've often complained of.

They will be missed.

So will fields of fireflies in June.

My little white house is calling me.

Tucked between two big blue houses.

Shaded by a handsome maple.

The cracked walkway

is for my feet.

The sounds of my big little city

will welcome me.

Your lips-

my neck-

I grow weak.

You said perhaps

your new favorite color

is phthalo green.

You laughed

as we played with the dogs

in the sun.

You remembered something

you said wrong

in French class-

it was a thing about the rain.

You rubbed my knee-

where my corduroys had worn.

You said I need new pants.

I said these do fine.

I asked what you said

in French class.

You put your forehead to mine

and said-

It is raining strawberries.

I spent New Year's Eve

with you-

and Chinese takeout-

we shared with Kill Bill Vol. 1.

You let me know more than once

it was your favorite movie-

one you watched a hundred times.

You-

were one of my favorite people.

I was always in awe of you-

you told me the same.

You sat me in the chair

that cost you three thousand dollars to refinish.

I was honored-

though you always sat me there.

And we tried and failed

to take a single good photo of us that night.

We laughed at our skills-

and the dog named Sasha

who watched our night.

I wish I'd stayed longer.

I'm glad I came.

I loved you madly.

I miss you terribly.

I am not the same.

What a

horrendously

beautiful

balancing act.

I rang the bell

as we entered the church.

I rang that bell.

I had an appreciation

of a sound that wandered

the grounds.

That spoke release.

A sound of deliverance

shouted to the crowd.

I am lost

to stillness-

lost

to starlight-

lost

to you.

Lost

to a lake

hungry

for my name.

And I-

am hungry

for all she holds.

This

is where I come from.

For this I am proud.

These

are the sounds

of my bones

and the songs

of my heart.

It's all been said.

There is no magic in this repetition.

No music for this dance.

No merriment

marking these words-

these sighs.

Each season knows them by heart.

The weight of them make the branches

groan-

and coyotes shriek.

And. I. Am. Tired.

Friends, and former lovers-

and new love-

meet here.

In this awkward union.

As I say good night

to things

that should be put to bed.

I'm going back-

back to the city.

To feel the sounds she makes.

to hear her morning groans

as she breaks awake.

To know the time of day

by the whistle at the shipyard.

And the bell at the church

on 5th.

To brush her sidewalks

in summer

when it rains.

And push past her citizens

doing the same.

To stare at streetlights-

my alternate stars.

We take our chances when

        f

        i

        s

        h

        i

        n

        g.

Yet we fish.

For food-

for hope-

for love.

For company.

To find ourselves.

To lose ourselves.

For the simple joy

in ripples we make-

in becoming the same.

Serenade in blue and white-

a serenade to you and me-

and the night.

Something undeniable-

unexpected-

unexplained.

And here we are

as friends.

Cheers-

to the blues and whites in life.

Cheers to you and me-

separate by country-

separate by birth.

United by poems

and chance-

and humor.

Here's to poetic-

sarcastic-

know-it-all-isms.

Here's to Boca.

Here's to Bukowski.

Here's to you-

and here's to me.

I'm back-

back in the city

Feeling the sounds she makes.

Hearing her morning groans

as she breaks awake.

I know the time of day

by the whistle at the shipyard.

And the bell at the church

on 5th.

I brush her sidewalks

in familiar ease

when it rains.

I push past her citizens doing the same.

And I stare now at streetlights-

instead of stars.

I sit-

on concrete steps of my own-

watching the red lights blinking

on a baby powder blue crane.

And I tuck myself

gently

into a small white frame

under a kind maple.

I'm craving simplicity-

and colors that let me breathe.

So carry me down Fourth Avenue-

horse drawn-

in a hearse of my own.

One I'll borrow for an hour

to take me down the streets of town.

I will dance to the sounds

of hooves on pavement-

and sing in colors of the sky.

I will shake awake

my big little city

in ordinary sounds.

I will cheer the weight of her buildings-

bricks profound.

I will laud the people of my city-

every passer-by.

I'll salute the people-

and my city-

and laud them with a cry.

I will split the streets

in sounds unheard.

I will crack my city open-

and I will be free.

There are songs I will never sing again-

not in full.

There are notes of me I'll leave

on the tops of Queen Anne's lace-

the wings of fireflies.

The cries of cranes that April brings-

to the maples on that ridge.

And songs I don't yet know.

I'll learn them with each step and season-

each sigh of my city.

I'll learn them as I go.

How the bell sounds on Sundays

from the church on Fifth-

how sounds call for attention on Sunday-

reaching for my street.

And the shipyard hum-

one that never stops.

The gray and black striped cat waiting on my stoop-

curious for a friend.

The Tuesday roar and then squeal

of a garbage truck we all agree to feed-

neighborhood offerings-

passing once again, a patient green couch

still waiting to be moved.

I don't know

that I can love you properly.

Not how you need.

My feet are dirty

and my house is clean.

I live barefoot

from a day in April

until the first freeze.

And I love.

I eat oatmeal or bagels-

or yogurt for breakfast-

or yogurt when I please.

I do not own a microwave.

Don't ask me for my reasons.

And I love.

I will never compromise

coffee at midnight.

I drink it

from necessity and joy.

Sometimes I'll choose tea.

Joy is found eye to eye in August grass

with a dog or two.

And I love.

Even

in November-

when grass can be seen-

all I want

are shoeless days-

and nights to write-

filled with heart

and little food.

And I love.

I may set you down

with my food-

and let you wilt

with my love for words.

But I promise

I will write

poetically

of that neglect.

I will write beautifully

of a life rendered.

And I love.

I bought two chairs

for five dollars each.

And a fistful of nails

for their wobbly wooden legs.

I need somewhere sturdy

to sit.

Because today-

my legs are not steady.

A gallon

of paint in a color

called slate.

A brush-

and a head

full of thoughts.

Thoughts to nail down.

I sent a text that said

we need to talk soon.

I hope you don't mind

the color

of my words.

I hope I hold.

Tell me what you thought today-

on the way to your very own knowing.

Of the things that buzzed in your head-

I could see the excitement of the perfect photo to be had.

And the flowers

that screamed for you to squeeze them-

on the way to the little white church

in Fish Creek.

The cedars that should have fallen

ages ago-

held by thoughts

of the people who now live as plaques

on a stone wall.

At least they are remembered.

Their names kept by the wall-

and the curious wanderers to that space.

People like us.

The poets with a sensibility

to enter an open gate that called.

People like us-

the oddities who needed to pay homage

to benches in sunlight.

People like us-

who write about such things, and know better

than to sit on them.

                While I am alive-

                I will live

to the left-

                                    and to the right-

                of beige.

Come for me-

while I smell of sweat-

and of earth.

Of Sunday.

Of August.

Look for me-

in woods or fields-

facing west.

While my feet

are bare.

While they kiss

the warm of the soil.

I'm prone

to say yes-

if you find me there.

Speak of sleep.

Speak

of rain.

Write of skies

that cannot be tamed.

Write me

in a way

that reflects the shine

of light

on a spider's web

at 4:07 pm

on this Sunday-

when the sun

clears the droop

of the maple and clouds.

And I am left to these.

Think of me-

when the sun slows.

When the light

glows-

slanted

on fading marigolds.

When monarchs

viewing the horizon-

contemplate leaving.

And crickets go dark.

Think of me-

when the sumac browns.

When quieter ways

wash this tired town.

When an agreement

to surrender-

is an agreement

to walk familiar

with a friend.

Stevie Nicks

and I

wait for rain.

With skies

and with hearts

about to burst.

Spinning

with sunflowers-

counting hours-

kissing bees.

Courting an afternoon.

Singing in ways

bigger than fields

and clouds

can contain.

Go slow-

go easy-

go low.

On a Chesterfield

couch

in medium blue.

While drops

from muddy skies

touch a roof

made of tin.

Speak simply.

Speak true.

Speak

of Monday-

of us.

Of a curious shade

seldom seen.

To all the boys

I meant to kiss.

And all the summer beans

I missed.

To the stars

and flowers

that burned my eyes.

And the red wings

on dragonflies.

And to the fog

that held captive

a heart-

and a church-

and a field

for a season.

I call you friend.

Of you I write.

To you-

I yield.

I will call on you

again

when the soil is warmed

and my feet

are bare.

Let us state the obvious

my giraffe.

What the night whispers.

What the soil rubs

against the bellies

of our bare feet.

The love you seek-

the love-

you and I claim

we are made for-

we have.

We are.

We are planets in conjunction-

leaping rivers.

We are poets-

coaxing cats

from cabbage trees.

You are an English Kiwi-

and I, a Capricorn-

traveling time.

Considering

the human condition.

Planting words

as we walk.

We remember-

in bits.

Recalling who we are.

That we are the very same

as the maple-

the velvet curtains in green-

and the angry bluffs

anchoring a lake.

The universe.

And we manifest ourselves

in fits of expression.

In painting-

in poem.

In novel.

In music and verse.

We view ourselves

in such ways.

The things we celebrate-

we are.

And we

are made

of the color of clouds.

Fields of fog.

Bridges in rain.

And these are things to dance to.

A maple on Mathey

was the first

to heed the call.

The first-

to shake summer.

The first

to show-

that giving in

to rest-

that letting go

of a long held breath

was inevitable.

And it is agreed

that this dance

between friends-

is quite

a handsome thing.

I rival the winds today

with my thoughts.

My heart is scattered-

and comes in bouts-

like the rain on my windshield.

Enough to feel.

Not enough to wipe away.

I rival the sounds

of the truck delivering tires.

And the sounds of my tire being changed-

split wide my head.

No sir-

my name is not Debbie.

The last owner of my car.

I want to ask him what she was like.

I almost do.

A young man walks by carrying tires.

I leave my thoughts

in that garage-

exchanging them

for the smell

of rubber

and oil-

and rain

and rain.

She calls.

And we are bound.

To a poem.

A steady repetition-

a rendition of sound.

And we are found

in cognition-

and awe-

of the primitive.

And the noble.

We look to the bluffs

held by cedar webs.

And we look to the horizon.

To skies in gray.

And to the seasons-

setting down the sun.

Feeding a lake that is hungry.

And we are stayed

in these days-

willingly.

We live-

our souls

crashed to her shores.

A cottage with a red door-

and a cement stoop.

Under the probe

of a streetlight-

and the hearts of friends.

A simple mess called home.

There were days we loved-

and did not know the other.

Days we loved-

and needed the other.

Nights-

That never stood still.

I am still tonight.

Marking dough.

In thumbprint reflections-

accumulated spells.

The last of the apple stores

burnt on hope.

Of all the others-

I stayed the length

of your youth.

I love you.

I do.

You and your Aries moon.

Your quick tongue-

a goodnight bid

an hour too soon.

An hour-

after 6:49 pm.

I smile.

I bid you the same.

The season dresses us-

just as she said.

We do not protest-

either of us-

to these muted nights

we attend.

We do not protest-

to a breath

that lets us

find our dreams.

I found you again.

and you found me.

And so it goes.

This dance we dance-

circling something

we touched once.

The uncharted familiar.

You said you know me.

I smiled-

and you do.

You called my presence

mesmerizing.

And I called you beautiful-

and smart-

that's what you are.

I think we'd fit each other

well.

Like I said-

yours

is a face

I cannot shake.

I loved you-

on that chair in the bookstore-

and on my sofa

in afternoon light.

And us-

beaming.

almost touching.

I asked you for another thought.

I never asked for the stars.

I never asked

to be in your arms that night.

You never asked me why.

And I-

I've got nothing

to compare you to-

to measure you by.

I stretch my arms

to the ceiling today.

And think of you.

In March

I tore down the ceiling

that held your name-

it was the sky.

I pressed my arms against odds.

In patience

I counted the days.

Like the sun, you circled back.

And like the moon-

I'd follow.

Though not always.

Some days I'd forget you.

Sometimes, your name.

I built my cottage in July-

ignoring August

as I always have.

Shining

in my big little city.

In September I was strong.

October came, pouring leaves-

peeling what the season shaped.

Dressing me in her fancy-

scratching paint.

Conquering me-

returning your name.

You asked

what I thought the pull was-

the force behind it.

I say marry me.

And after the wedding

I'll explain the bedding

of two souls.

There is something that says

do not look away-

the coyote

smashed in sunlight

tells us to stay.

To find the you and me

in this thing we carry.

You challenge me-

I like the electric mind

behind a face I melt for.

I text hello.

I still melt for you today.

I said no

to you last night-

because I so badly

wanted to say yes.

I breathed in Sunday-

and I thought of you.

I ate yogurt with my coffee-

and only wanted you.

I paced my living room-

looking

to where you should be seated.

Where I tell you

exactly what this means.

Where your words

challenge mine-

though your Virgo eyes

and brown skin agree.

Where we resurrect a temple

and worship you and me.

Where we own Sunday.

Where on Sunday-

like scared gods-

the hours are ours.

I learned the alphabet game from you

tonight.

You learned the sound

of my heart-

consistent-

no matter the closeness of us.

And the sound

of my vascular system.

You swore you could hear

the blood running

through my veins.

I carefully learned

the curve of your ear.

And with your finger-

you drew the shape

of the evening

on my chest.

There was a first

and second

and a third kiss.

We stopped at the letter x-

falling asleep

holding hands.

I am intrigued.

Unsettle me.

I count on you

to find my door.

To cross the city streets-

to make your way

down North Fourth Avenue.

To press down intentions

with every step-

in this first snow.

My big little city

is suddenly still

for the first time all season.

I feel you near.

I can hear you-

against this quiet.

I expect to see your face

on my stoop.

To greet you with a nod.

I'm watching this snow

from my window.

I'm expecting you.

I'll wait.

My eyes

are not the color of the sky.

Or of the hungry lake

that knows my name.

They are the bluffs

that kiss such things-

that watch such things-

that taste such things.

They are the soil and stone

that make such things.

They are the color of truth.

They hold-

even as you and she dance.

You wander in on waves

in your way.

And I hold.

You dare come to shore

from time to time.

You look for something

firmer than water

to dance with-

you claim only I can calm you.

And with the brown of my eyes-

I believe this to be true.

You were on your way.

I wanted to see you.

My text, however, read-

> *Is a moment with you worse than not seeing you at all?*
>
> *Have a beautiful day.*

I was intent on keeping you at bay.

Off my street and heart.

You pressed your feet on both.

I felt that.

I heard you in the silence of the snow.

Especially in that silence.

You shattered that with your face.

Fuck you for that.

We greeted with a hug.

It had been seven months.

For seven months

I could not shake the thought of you.

Eyes so wide

and lips that pulled me in

with every word.

I tried not to stare.

I tried.

We spoke of rank and caliber-

I said you measure.

We spoke of missing days

and lingering feelings-

we felt the same.

I said you belong here-

that there is space for you here.

You smiled-

you said you knew.

I asked if I could kiss you.

I asked with the brown of my eyes

if I could kiss you.

The brown of yours said yes.

Your smile-

and our skin touching-

said yes.

Your words said

not just yet.

Skies exhale-

and my eyes

wish you here.

My heart-

my skin-

my breath

that have become a sigh-

wishes you here.

Dogs bark

outside my window-

and even they know.

You dare me

to walk your words.

As always

they lead me

back to your lips.

The hidden parts of you-

I've asked to see.

You tell me they are dark-

and some, not beautiful.

That perhaps they'd scare.

And I say, show me all of you.

Your sins, your joys, your scars.

I recognize the shadows behind your eyes.

You pull me, as the lake does.

And I am bound.

You and she, know my name.

You and she repeat my name in waves that kiss my feet.

I pace the shores, writing poems in sand-

shouting them over a space so grand

they feel meaningless.

I feel you hear me.

Perhaps you'll grow tired of sleeping under water.

You have a brilliance I wish you'd see.

Let me tell you-

face to face-

eye to eye-

nose to nose-

heart to heart.

Let me tell you.

Like the bluffs, I'll wait.

All I know

is that I needed to find you-

I needed to know you were okay.

So this is your love poem.

You are worth my heart.

Worth fighting for.

Worth wondering about.

Worth a night

driving through the Algoma fog.

And I found you.

I found you.

I think I confused your dad-

knocking at your door.

I don't care.

I'm confused too.

All I know

is that your face and name

feel good to my heart.

That is all I need to know.

I learned

that you don't love the roads in winter-

how you feel less safe when they are taken by her.

I learned tonight of your mother-

you said she died two years ago.

Your breath and lungs

spoke of how you miss her so.

How the absence of her fells so big.

Still.

That yes, I confused your father when I knocked on your door.

I drove through fog to find you.

I had to find you.

You have to know.

I learned

unless you can see the words written on a chalkboard-

they are of no use to you.

That the sound of chalk during a lecture-

even covered in music

without a clear view-

is a no.

That in searching for songs to show me-

you get lost along the way.

That MGK we agree on-

aesthetically he pleases-

and musically, he is a god.

I learned

your nephew is older than you

by about fifteen months.

You whispered to take his words

with a grain of salt.

He is likeable, I whispered back.

Agreeable you said, is a word that better suits.

That you love sweets

just as much as me.

And offered me cookies-

endlessly.

That bread and butter are alright-

and so are noodles with beans.

Not the crunch of toast.

It's something I will note.

I learned

that you can't imagine a life so big

without the words.

That words are spells-

but sometimes it's just a feeling.

Sometimes you just know.

I feel this too.

My heart, and your feet have met.

I like them there.

It's where you wrote your name.

Our thoughts and eyes always meet with ease.

As did our arms-

my hand to the chest of you.

The other in your pocket as we slept.

MGK sang us lullabies.

I learned

that you will trust me in holding your hair-

as you fix it once again

to place under your blue bandana.

You honored us both

in allowing yourself to be held-

unguarded as you.

This thing called you-

is made more tangible.

We strung affections

on silence-

on the night.

Now-

a bit firmer than water-

more decided.

Though as easy to hold as sand-

you are a man at shore.

I learned the sound

love makes-

traveling seventeen miles

and twenty-three minutes

in the dark.

Laugh-

or don't.

I loved you.

And I am scarred.

Happily-

or not.

Marked in proper-

your feet-

my heart.

I know now

the weight

of my worth.

I know now

what I want.

I am no longer afraid

to seek those things.

The things

that bring me joy.

Made in the USA
Middletown, DE
03 January 2023